VAN DYCK

FONTANA UNESCO ART BOOKS

Edited by Peter Bellew

Van Dyck

·David Piper

COLLINS *in association with* UNESCO

There are qualities, or moods, of the human imagination that can seem positively to have been invented, rather than merely visually defined, by certain great artists, even though once revealed they seem essential. Before Giorgione, there is no witness of quite that haunting, bewitched pastoral voluptuousness, which now Giorgione's name by itself is sufficient to evoke, and which is an integral element of European culture. Van Dyck, if less obviously than Giorgione, is one of these mood-establishing masters, and without him a certain strain of melancholic elegance is unimaginable.

Though the persistence of this strain throughout his work, from the first precocious self-portrait, painted in Antwerp at the age of fourteen (and now in Vienna) until his last works before his premature death in London in 1641, is undeniable, art historians divide him not without reason into four parts—the Van Dyck of the first Antwerp period, of the Italian period, of the second Antwerp period and of the final English one.

He was born in Antwerp in 1599; the social status of his family is somewhat argued over, but he seems to have come from a merchant stock of middling condition. His formal education, in the liberal arts and sciences, cannot have been very extensive for by the time he was only ten he was apprenticed to a now largely forgotten painter, van Balen. He was beyond doubt precocious, for by 1618, when he was entered as a master in the Antwerp Guild of Painters, he had already a considerable reputation. By 1619 indeed he was working with Rubens in Antwerp, and though described as an *allievo* or pupil, was more likely a true if junior collaborator with his celebrated elder. At the end of the same year his own travels began, and he left for England, wooed away from Flanders by the first connoisseur and collector, in the modern sense, in England —the Earl of Arundel. Something however seems to have gone wrong on this occasion, and though he certainly worked for the king (James I), his stay was brief, and early in 1621 he was back again in Antwerp, only to leave for Italy in the autumn of the same year. There he was to stay for some five and a half years. His immediate destination was Genoa, and it is above all with the rich and aristocratic patrons of Genoa that his Italian sojourn is associated, although the primary Italian inspiration in his work came, even before he had set eyes upon Italy, from the Venetian masters, and amongst them, always and above all, from Titian. He now visited Rome, Bologna, Florence, and Venice itself, but mostly he was in Genoa.

In the autumn of 1627 he returned to Antwerp, and there for the next four years was established, on occasion, as the leading painter. On occasion, because the overriding genius of Rubens was still dominant in Antwerp, radiating thence like a sun over all Northern Europe. But Rubens was frequently away at this time, restless perhaps after the death of his wife, Isabella Brant, and finding distraction in his subsidiary career as a prince of diplomats—he was away on diplomatic errands most notably, for the English at least, in London in 1629-30. There is anyway no evidence that Van Dyck suffered from any lack of work at this time; he was court painter to Isabella, the regent of the Netherlands, and his success was formidable. So much so indeed that it is doubtless at this time that he began, under an excess of patronage, to organise his work on the pattern of a large studio as practised by Rubens, delegating much of the more mechanical processes to assistants. But even so it may be that even in Antwerp there was not really room—whether a practical room or a psychological one—for two such eminences as Rubens and Van Dyck, and this may well have decided his migration to England in 1632.

In London his welcome was almost that of a prince, for

Lucas Vorsterman. c. 1631. Drawing, 24,3 x 17,6 cm. Fitzwilliam Museum, Cambridge.

Charles I of England was avid for art. Rubens had stayed in London little more than a matter of months, although he had—amid his diplomatic businesses—accepted the commission from the king for what was to prove the only major decoration in baroque painting in England, the great ceiling in Inigo Jones's Banqueting House at Whitehall Palace. But Rubens had gone, so Van Dyck, by now almost Rubens's sibling in international reputation, was all the more to be cherished by the English. He was granted a house in Blackfriars, a golden chain, a pension; three months after his arrival he was knighted—an honour never before granted to any painter resident in England, though already granted to the transient Rubens. For the remainder of his short life, Van Dyck was based on England; he was away in Antwerp for almost a year in 1634, and then during the last eighteen months of his life, after Rubens had died and the whole of Europe seemed open to Van Dyck as his fit and proper successor as the greatest painter in the world, he was back in Antwerp and in Paris, clearly investigating where his best prospects might lie. It may well be that, had he lived, he would have re-established himself on the Continent, but when, in December 1641, death interrupted him he was in London. In his will, he asked to be buried in St. Paul's Cathedral and there, at the king's order, his tomb was duly erected. The tomb itself vanished in the fire of 1666 that destroyed old St. Paul's, but his fame did not. He was only forty-two years old when he died.

Consideration of Van Dyck as painter can only start with Rubens. It is Van Dyck's fate always to have to be considered in the light of Rubens, as the moon in the light of the sun, or the second generation of the millionaire dynasty in the shadow of the founder and creator of the fortune. Van Dyck was heir to the revolution, to the literal reformation of Northern European art in the terms of the Baroque that Rubens had revealed to all Northern Europe on his return from Italy in 1608. The effect of this revolution in painting, technically described as the yielding of the Mannerist style to the Baroque, was to release the art as if from a profound spiritual neurosis and physical cramp into a dynamic convulsion of movement. That is of course greatly to oversimplify, but art historians can tend sometimes in their analysis of the means by which this was achieved—by the new sophistication of rhythm, for example, or the opening up of the picture space by sharp recessions and dramatic diagonal movement—to understress the obvious, which is that the effect, certainly for contemporaries, was a new intoxicating revelation of the naturalistic possibilities in painting: of its power of sheer illusionism. In this mode the vitality of Rubens was such that he seemed to impose his own vision on nature, onto the visible world, with such force and irresistible conviction that his colleagues could not help but find him there. Van Dyck was no exception, and he moreover, in his beginnings, worked in actual close collaboration with Rubens, so that in certain paintings on which they both worked it is still impossible to say with certainty where Rubens ends and Van Dyck begins. Certain other pictures tend to be disputed between the two, and others, certainly by Van Dyck, are so closely modelled on Rubens that it might seem more valid to consider them in terms of Rubens rather than of Van Dyck. Such a state of things is of course normal, perhaps inevitable, in the relationship between an older master of genius and a much younger one still in search of his own identity. What is extraordinary is that Van Dyck, at this tender age, still in his teens, was not entirely swamped by Rubens; but he was not, and here and there in the early work, done before he was twenty-two, he is visible, if still outshone by Rubens, as a clearly distinct personality in his own right. By the time he was twenty-one, in 1620, he was reported to be already producing work that " was beginning to be valued almost as highly as that of his master ".

Thus in an early *Self-portrait* (the version in Munich is perhaps of late 1622) we find him already lucidly defined. I suppose the most astonishing quality of this painting, for so young a painter, is its sheer virtuosity. But the characterisation is very revealing: that slight hint of appeal, though already very far from being posed without

The Betrayal of Christ. Drawing, 24,1 x 20,9 cm. Musée du Louvre, Paris. (Photo Giraudon.)

confidence, will vanish, but the extraordinary elegance of grace will persist, and so too will the nervous sensitivity that informs the drawing and the movement of the paint, so characteristically here most markedly in the hands. And the sumptuousness will stay; this is no labouring artisan, but a princeling of the arts who will come to look upon the highest in any court at his own level. Typically, when in Rome, he held aloof from the many lesser Flemish artists who led there a rather disorderly and Bohemian way of life; they called him " il cavaliere ". Rubens too was a prince amongst painters, but the comparison of any self-portrait by Rubens with one by Van Dyck will bring out a train of languor in the younger man, a softer and more feminine talent that can even verge dangerously close to sentimentality. Not that I would for a moment suggest that femininity is the equivalent of sentimentality, and indeed many of Van Dyck's early works will dispel any doubt there might be of his ambitiousness and ability to design on a grand scale. For example, a design that he repeated several times, the *Betrayal of Christ*, or the *Kiss of Judas*, which dates from about 1620 and of which the best-known version is in the Prado: the very teeming-ness of that design reflects Rubens, but in spirit, with its rush of broken and flickering colour, it is already inspired more by Italian, Venetian examples, and it has a dramatic and atmospheric mystery that Rubens never encompassed, in which the solid forms seem to flow, almost dissolve, in colour. The *St. Martin Dividing his Cloak*, more monumental in conception, still has this same twin allegiance—in the drawing of the beggar, in that powerful naked back—to Rubens, while the design for the horseman is borrowed from Titian; and if the slight cramping of the whole composition within the picture space is typically Van Dyck of this period, so essentially too is the silvery elegance of it, the sophisticated grace and balance of gesture—all from a man of not more than twenty-two.

While Van Dyck was, to the end, to acknowledge in his work his enduring debt to the inspiration of Rubens and of Titian, it was in the six years he spent in Italy that he reached his maturity and established his own inimitable mastery. Sensitive as a chameleon to his surroundings, both physical and spiritual, he shifted his key of colour when he arrived in Italy; its texture becomes at once more broken and richer, and can in some paintings glow like a banked fire. In his religious paintings, he evolved gradually a compromise between the strenuously aspiring saints of the Flemish tradition and the sweeter gestures, the sometimes near-morbid ecstasies, of certain Italian painters, and his Madonnas, in their melting femininity and gentleness, seem near relations of those of Guido Reni. More importantly perhaps, in terms of his contribution to man's vision of man, he began in Italy that great series of portraits, so often full-length, for which he is now best remembered. With dignity, with gravity, with a formidable yet not a chilling reticence, he painted the Genoese aristocracy from the point of view of a fellow-aristocrat. It was so to speak a revelation of the visual essence of aristocracy. The famous portrait of the *Marchesa Elena Grimaldi-Cattaneo*, in Philadelphia,—this is how one imagines any feminine aristocrat worthy of her rank must feel herself essentially to be, yet did not know it till Van Dyck showed her—aloof and formally regal, but endowed with an elegance and grace that are infinitely seductive. Her clothes, the Italian light itself, the glowing colour, become almost the vestments of a ceremonial order of society, become indeed almost sacramental. It shows Van Dyck's eclectic genius at its highest, for while it is an ungrudging tribute to Italian precedent (to Veronese in this case), it is also in its dream-like conviction and its tall and fluent dignity, wholly Van Dyck's, and one of the greatest pageant portraits ever painted. It was also in Italy, that in portraits like the *White Boy*, or, still more intimately and understandingly, the little girl with the resonant title of *Marchesa Clelia Cattaneo*, he announced a theme on which he has no peer, except perhaps Velasquez: the intimations of aristocracy in children upon whose fragile shoulders worldly greatness is inexorably to be thrust.

On Van Dyck's return to Flanders in 1627, his response to the northern light was immediate; the colour shifts key, becomes cooler, shimmering from the gleaming black in which his Flemish sitters are almost uniformly clad. The social range of these sitters seems wider than it had been in Italy, and their diversity is reflected acutely in the diversity of Van Dyck's characterisations of them; but even when drawn from the bourgeoisie, they appear as members of a rich and ordered society of great distinction and elegance. Antwerp, though already declining from its great period of mercantile predominance, was in fact still very much such a society; the contrasts with the far more individualistic bourgeois communities of neighbouring Protestant Holland is very marked. In Holland, at the time that Van Dyck was working in Antwerp, the young Rembrandt was beginning to forge his own style with which he would later explore the mysteries of individual human identity—an essentially Protestant one, held clear of the shadow of encroaching darkness as if by sheer will-power; the image of man alone with himself, searching, uncertain if he is made in the image of God, but determined to find out. Van Dyck's investigation was into a quite different order of identity; while the faces of his sitters are recorded with scrupulous particularity and rare conviction, their total personalities are heroically idealised by means of gesture, pose and costume, and by the grandeur of their mundane setting, and not least by the fluent magnificence of the painter's style. The emphasis is on the social identity; though melancholy invest the features, as it often does in Van Dyck, it is usually secondary to a celebration of felicity in material well-being. One of the most remarkable spheres in which Van Dyck exploited this idealising vision was in his recording of the persons of his fellow artists, that ambitious series of studies which form the backbone of the great suite of etchings known as the *Iconographie* and which include some of his most seductive and sensitive characterisations. Implicitly, these studies reject any conception of the artist as mere artisan, and mirror him instead as man of high breeding and culture, elegant, self-assured and easy, as *virtuoso*: an aristocrat of intellect who is the peer of any aristocrat of mere blood. Yet, if, in his presentation of his sitters, there is always a very public aspect, this does not mean that undertones of intimacy are necessarily absent. During his second Antwerp period, Van Dyck was establishing his mastery in another *genre*, that of the double portrait. The double portrait, in lesser hands than those of Van Dyck, can only too easily be a mere description of two bodies juxtaposed, but with him it can become almost a portrait of empathy between two human beings made visible. One of the most haunting of his essays in this kind is the painting of a man wife (traditionally known as *Mytens and his wife*, but the man resembles the Dutch painter Cornelis van Poelenbergh very closely) at Woburn Abbey. The relationship, the give and take between the two characters, is established by the most precise subtlety of design and handling of the brush, but from the echoes there wells out, inexhaustible, the aura of a gravely serene domestic affection, welded by time and habit into a harmony stronger, it seems, even than time and habit. It is redolent of the most profound intimacy, yet it finds its natural, inevitable expression in ceremony.

In Flanders, too, Catholic patronage still gave the artist scope for development of large religious compositions, and he produced a number of baroque altarpieces in the full-scale Tridentine tradition; if in these too there is the same cooling of the colour key as in the portraits, there is also an even more assured mastery of composition that derives from Van Dyck's unrelenting study of the old masters in Italy. For some, what may seem the blatancy of emotion, as in the Ellesmere *Virgin and Child*, so typical of the religious painting of the Counter-Reformation, can be initially unsympathetic, but underlying it is the most unsentimental grasp of form. He painted also a number of heroic, mythological, or poetic, subjects; amongst them, in its teeming invention and movement, the *Rinaldo and Armida* at Baltimore is one of the most successful. This was painted in 1629, and came to Charles I of England, to whet still further that monarch's desire to entice Van Dyck to England.

It may be in fact that, in moving to England in 1632, Van Dyck hoped to be rewarded by a generous and am-

Queen Henrietta Maria. c. 1638. Canvas, 210 x 130 cm. Windsor Castle. (Photo Anderson-Giraudon.)

bitious patronage that would enable him to exploit to the utmost his gift for large pageant-like decoration. Charles I was the first monarch in England who qualified in his own right as a discriminating and learned patron of the arts, and he was passionately concerned to lift his island, hitherto as far as the arts were concerned relegated to the status of a somewhat retarded and provincial appendage on the fringe of Europe, to a position of parity with the most sophisticated of Continental courts. To this end he was busy acquiring not only great collections of old masters but also the services of the finest living masters whom he could attract to England. But if Van Dyck had dreams of creating a great series of decorations (such as those in the Louvre done by Rubens for Maria de' Medici), he was to be disappointed. He did in fact paint a number of religious and heroic pictures, but the prevailing temper of England was Protestant, and outside the limited circle of the court, and particularly that of Charles's French-born and Catholic queen, Henrietta Maria, religious painting was anathema; hardly any of the ones he did have survived. Charles's ambitions of splendour were also circumscribed. Van Dyck's stay in England coincided with an uneasy interlude in English history, when the king dismissed Parliament, and the embryonic traditions of democracy that had grown up under Elizabeth I, in favour of a personal absolutism. For a decade, before the outbreak of civil war in 1642, the surface glittered magnificently, but beneath it lay deep unease and the beginnings of revolt; also, though Charles could manage in many ways quite well without Parliament, the difficulties of raising money without Parliamentary authority, in the form of taxes, proved very stubborn indeed. Patronage of the arts depended like so many things on money, and there survives even a bill from Van Dyck to Charles I, for paintings delivered, on which the king in his own hand has marked down the prices. The artist was inevitably thrown back on portraits for his livelihood. In portraiture, however, the demand—and throughout his stay Van Dyck catered almost exclusively for the circle immediately about the king himself—was loaded with more splendid opportunities than had existed in Antwerp, either in its merchant society or from the patronage of the regent who had by then withdrawn almost entirely into her religious order. The England that he burst upon had acquired no comparable artistic phenomenon since Holbein, and the portraiture to which they were accustomed before Van Dyck was provincial and relatively old-fashioned, the somewhat rigid presentation of the sitter as if stuffed for posterity, still inhibited by the tradition of stiff and smooth effigies made fashionable by earlier court painters. In contrast, the transformation or apotheosis that Van Dyck offered his clients when they entered his studio must have seemed little short of miraculous. A contemporary English poet even referred to Van Dyck's studio as his " beauty-shop ". The procedure, as reported by a great devotee of Van Dyck's, the collector Jabach, could seem perhaps not so far removed from that of a successful beauty-salon, both in its polish and its efficiency.

" Having made appointments with his sitters, he never worked more than an hour at each portrait, whether sketching it or finishing it, and when the clock warned him the hour was over, he rose, made a bow to his sitter, to intimate that enough had been done for that day, and made arrangements for another sitting. Then his servants came to clean his brushes, and brought him another palette, ready for the next sitter. He thus worked at many portraits in one day, and with extraordinary rapidity. Having slightly sketched a portrait, he placed his sitter in the attitude he had previously arranged, and with black and white chalk, on grey paper, he sketched the figure and dress, which he designed in a grand style, and with exquisite taste. This drawing he gave to able assistants, who afterwards copied it, with the help of the dresses lent, at his request, by his sitter. When his pupils had painted, to the best of their ability, the drapery in the picture, Van Dyck touched lightly over it, and in a very short time, with his knowledge, produced the truth and art which we admire in his pictures. For the hands, he had in his employ people of both sexes who served him as models..."[*]

Such was the production technique that Van Dyck

brought to perfection in his last years in England—to perfection at least of production method. To modern notions, it may seem somewhat repellant; uncomfortably close to mass-production and the factory belt. And quite certainly the end-product, in these later years, tended to suffer, and the quality of Van Dyck's English portraits is notoriously uneven. There are examples of portraits which, while they are stamped unmistakably as Van Dyck designs, do not exist in what one could orthodoxly call an original version, for the simple reason that there never was an original, in the sense of a painting completed entirely by the master's own hand. For the seventeenth-century client, however, it was perfectly acceptable (though there are instances of Van Dyck's patrons, as there are of Rubens's, insisting that a work be entirely from the master's own hand). For posterity it means that there are good Van Dycks and bad Van Dycks, but what is important is the quality of the good ones, and they are not rare. In fact, the difference between bad and good is very slight, a matter, it can be, of micromillimetres, yet also the difference between life and death: the individual movement of the great painter's brush, not tracing but discovering the contour; the flicker, the hesitation, articulating the overall design as breath informs the living body—and the movement of Van Dyck's paint, the nervous almost electric sensitivity of his drawing, these offer some of the most seductive pleasures in all European painting.

Yet for most of his clients—the English ones at this time mostly relatively unsophisticated in connoisseurship —it will have been the grand design that mattered. Van Dyck's predecessors had produced the English as if in airless display boxes, posed much as upright effigies, and anyway dead. With Van Dyck, the windows open, a breeze moves through the room, draperies move in it and the light itself seems to stream with it; this movement is stressed usually by strong diagonal emphasis in the composition. The sitters' clothes are relatively loose about the body, particularly the women's. The total impression was, for the clients, certainly of a startling illusionism; when their portraits were finished, they had confronting them an almost breathing image of themselves. This would be surprising enough in itself, but the reflection, besides being lifelike, was of course also into the bargain flattering. Van Dyck (as I have already intimated earlier) was not a base flatterer; that is, there is little evidence to suggest that he flattered by the manipulation of the sitter's features— by smoothing them out or minimising blemishes, for example. The only case recorded is that of Queen Henrietta Maria, who was long known to a niece only from a portrait by Van Dyck; when they actually met the niece was disillusioned, finding that the queen's teeth stuck out like " defence-works ". But I doubt if this was characteristic, and suspect that the reaction of another English female subject was more normal. She was distressed when she saw her own portrait, finding it very stout (as if " done of the wind's puffing "), but nevertheless was forced to add: " But truly I think it is like the original." But whether his portraits were like or not, whether at times he was a little over-polite to his sitter's vanity in them, these are now academic points of no great moment; his real flattery of them was achieved in other ways, and especially by the absorbing of their ephemeral individual human frailty into a grand and enduring pictorial design— into a work of art. He could thus bewitch a sitter most simply into immortality, just a straightforward head and shoulders, by the magical mastery of his paint—in the larger designs by the magnificence and the movement of the composition, and not unseldom by a sort of built-in cross-reference to earlier masterpieces. Thus his *Earl of Strafford* at Petworth refers in design and pose back to a military portrait by Titian, and this reference back works, not like a mere imitation, but as a supporting quotation from an earlier and heroic authority. Van Dyck did not copy from the Italians (though his experience of them, particularly of Titian, was greatly refreshed in England where they were most richly represented in Charles I's collection); rather, he rediscovered and so revitalised their known poses and compositions in the living sitter in front of him. In fact his characterisation of the Englishman has proved seminal; it has even been claimed that in a visual sense Van Dyck created, if not the English gentleman, at least the English aristocrat. It is quite true that if, in an English country house, you survey the portraits of its successive owners through the eighteenth and nineteenth centuries you will find again and again recurring that typical Van Dyck cast of features, high and proud as houses with shut windows, and a little equine, and like Queen Victoria, superbly uninterested in defeat.

With women, his successes are even more spectacular. One of his most ravishingly beautiful female portraits is the three-quarter length of the *Countess of Bedford* at Petworth, in its fluid glowing wealth of colour, its consummate drawing—the extension of the hand into the half-drawn-off glove is one of the most *virtuoso* passages of paint that Van Dyck ever managed. His vision of women answers that of the contemporary Cavalier poet, Robert Herrick, who celebrated " a sweet disorder in the dress ", rather than " when art is too precise in every part ". Not long after Van Dyck's death, his contemporary Sanderson, one of the first English writers on art, noted that he was the " first painter who e'er put ladies dress into a careless romance ", and it is true that his female portraits are the first fully feminine ones in England, as also that, more vulgarly, it is to his example that the long and undying tradition of the English " pin-up " portrait can be traced back. The *Countess of Bedford* hangs with three other Van Dyck portraits of famous beauties at Petworth, and they seem to have been together almost since they were painted, while they early became known to a wider public by engravings. Yet it is also true that their facial beauty is not falsely cosseted, and glamorised. If, for example, you isolate the face of the *Countess of Bedford* amidst the elegant splendour of paint with which Van Dyck's evokes her presence, you will find the features very far from pretty-pretty, and far perhaps from a modern conception of what constitutes beauty in a female face. The portrait as a whole breathes of femininity, of glamour, but it is the painting with which one might fall in love, not the sitter. The same contrast is visible in one of his finest female whole-lengths, the *Penelope, Lady*

Spencer at Althorp. She rises through that fall of pale blue satin almost like a fountain folding and unfolding upon itself; she has all the dizzy, precarious dignity of youth, and is poised, with that art in which Van Dyck has no equal, as it were between one movement and the next, breathing-still. A stillness of poise emphasized by the little dog jumping up at her side—and if you look closer to find what has excited the dog, you see it is a lizard, frozen on the stone; a lizard, the quickest thing on earth, that too will be gone should you blink. And yet amongst all this, the face, the defining individuality of the sitter, is observed scrupulously, a little plump as if still with some puppy-fat, a little heavy even, the face of a young English girl not quite certain enough of herself to be sure that she will be asked for the next dance and not have to sit it out.

It was then in portraiture that Van Dyck at his best achieved his masterpieces in his last years. There are however a few rare exceptions. In a number of drawings and water-colours (the connection of which with Van Dyck has been argued in the past but is now generally admitted), there is an extraordinary fresh and original apprehension of pure landscape that looks forward a century or more to the great burgeoning of the English water-colour school. And there are one or two subject pictures, most notably an allegory of *Cupid and Psyche* painted for Charles I and still in the Royal Collection—an echo of all that was best, most sensitive and most delicate in the poetic imagination of Charles's court. It is also an example of the extreme sensitivity of its painter to mood and atmosphere, a subduing of the Baroque into a more classicizing mode but with an elegance, both chaste and voluptuous, that is almost rococo. It was into paintings such as this that he had to sublimate the more plangently expressive sensuousness that had earlier informed his religious paintings such as the great *Lamentation* now in Munich. In that, the pose of the Christ is very close to that of Psyche, but the adaptation of mood and colour to the later subjects reflects exactly the mood and temper of the English imagination.

Charles I. Three Heads. 1636. Canvas, 83 x 100 cm. Windsor Castle.
(Copyright reserved.)

It is however the portraits that predominate, that stay
in the memory, and that have indeed become part of
English history. In one most important case, in fact, the
name of the artist is hardly to be dissociated from his
subject—King Charles I, whose true apotheosis is by Van
Dyck in the long series of portraits painted by him, a
triumphal and romantic verdict that not one of the count-
less subsequent inquisitions by historians into the short-
comings of Charles as monarch has been able to sabotage.
No king, not even Charles V by Titian, or Philip IV by
Velasquez, has been imaged in such variety of genius. The
enduring fascination of Van Dyck's portrait of Charles I
arises of course in part from the nature of the king's own

tragic destiny, and it may be that part of the melancholy that we now read into the king's features arises from hindsight, as we know the fate that was to overtake him on the scaffold on a bleak January day in 1649, when, condemned by his own subjects, his head fell to the executioner's axe. Yet though Van Dyck himself died eight years before the king, and before England's unease had broken out into civil war, there are ironies built into some of the portraits. The great equestrian portrait in the London National Gallery for example; this was carried out as homage to two masters, to the king himself and to Titian (we know from Bellori that it was painted in deliberate emulation of Titian's famous *Charles V at the Battle of Mühlberg*). It is indeed a grandiose celebration of Charles as warrior-king, yet, at the same time, in key with that peculiar decade of English history, it has a strangely unreal air. It is about pageantry rather than real war; no one would have dreamed of going into real action in that obsolete armour at the time it was painted. But Van Dyck painted Charles in many rôles—as warrior; as monarch robed; as a gentleman-king in that magical pastoral portrait in the Louvre. He painted him also three-in-one, the head portrayed from three different angles on one canvas, and it is this portrait, in close-up, that may persuade one that one is not inventing Charles's melancholy out of sentiment. The triple portrait was sent as a model for Bernini in Rome as " copy " for a marble bust, and an early story has it that the sculptor was so overcome by the overtones of doom in the face that he burst into tears. " A face fit to paint the Saviour from ", said an eighteenth-century Englishman, and it can seem that Van Dyck formulated the image of Charles the Martyr before the event. Van Dyck's rendering of Charles and his silk-swathed courtiers has indeed made that brief decade the most glamorous period of English history.

His achievement does not stop there. His style echoed on throughout Europe; in France particularly a crisp and flounced version of it was propagated through all the arts of Northern Europe from the example of the court paint-ers of Versailles, Largillière and Rigaud (who was advised by Le Brun not to go to study in Venice, but rather to stay at home and study " nature and Van Dyck "). But in England the artistic debt was overriding, and Van Dyck became the founding figure of the English school of painters, and its patron saint. " We shall all go to heaven ", said Gainsborough on his death-bed to Sir Joshua Reynolds, " and Van Dyck is of the company."

ILLUSTRATIONS

8

12

14

17

27

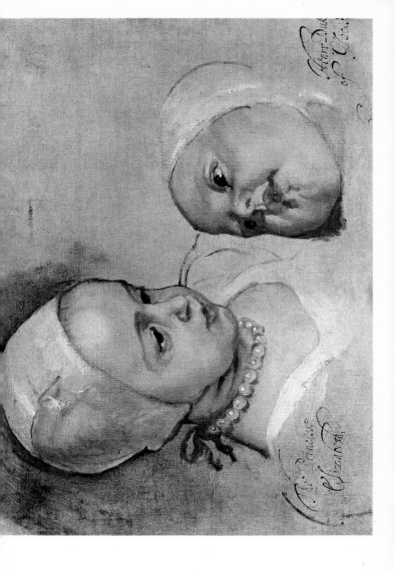

28

CONTENTS

BIBLIOGRAPHY

ADRIANI, Gert, *Anton Van Dyck, Italienisches Skizzenbuch*, Vienna, A. Schroll & Co., 1940.

CUST, Sir Lionel, *Anthony Van Dyck. An historical study of his life and work*, London, G. Bell & Sons, Ltd., 1900.

DELACRE, M., Recherches sur le rôle du dessin dans l'Iconographie de Van Dyck, *Mémoires de l'Académie Royale de Belgique*, 2e série, II, 4, Brussels, 1932.

DELACRE, M., Le Dessin dans l'œuvre de Van Dyck, *Mémoires de l'Académie Royale de Belgique*, 2e série, III, 1, Brussels, 1934.

GLÜCK, Gustav, *Van Dyck, Des Meisters Gemälde*, (Klassiker der Kunst), Stuttgart, Deutsche Verlaganstalt, 1931.

GLÜCK, Gustav, *Rubens, Van Dyck, und ihr Kreis*, Vienna, A. Schroll & Co., 1933.

GUIFFREY, Jules, *Antoine Van Dyck, sa vie et son œuvre*, Paris, A. Quantin, 1882.

JAFFÉ, Michael, *Van Dyck's Antwerp Sketchbook*, London, MacDonald & Co. Ltd., 1966.

MAUQUOY-HENDRICKX, Marie, *L'Iconographie d'Antoine Van Dyck*, Brussels, Académie Royale de Belgique, 1956.

PUYVELDE, Léon van, *La Peinture flamande du XVIIe siècle, Van Dyck*, Brussels-Amsterdam, Gründ, 1950.

VEY, Horst, *Die Zeichnungen Anton Van Dycks*, Brussels, Editions l'Arcade, 1962.

WHINNEY, Margaret; MILLAR, Oliver, *English Art 1625-1714*, Oxford, Clarendon Press, 1957.

* (p. 17) Translated from: ROGER DE PILES, *Cours de peinture par principes*, pp. 291-293, Paris, Jacques Estienne, 1708.

CONTENTS